HOPE & H

WHEN YOUR FRIEND DIES

HAROLD IVAN SMITH

Augsburg

MINNEAPOLIS

Other books in the Hope and Healing series:
When Your Parent Dies
When Your Spouse Dies
When Your Child Dies
When Your Baby Dies through Miscarriage or Stillbirth
When Your Child Loses a Loved One

WHEN YOUR FRIEND DIES

Copyright © 2002 Augsburg Fortress. All rights reserved. Except for brief quotations in critical articles or reviews, no part of this book may be reproduced in any manner without prior written permission from the publisher. Write to: Permissions, Augsburg Fortress, Box 1209, Minneapolis, MN 55440.

Large-quantity purchases or custom editions of this book are available at a discount from the publisher. For more information, contact the sales department at Augsburg Fortress, Publishers, 1-800-328-4648, or write to: Sales Director, Augsburg Fortress, Publishers, P.O. Box 1209, Minneapolis, MN 55440-1209.

Scripture passages are from the New Revised Standard Version of the Bible, copyright © 1946, 1952, 1971, 1989 by the Division of Christian Education of the National Council of the Churches of Christ in the USA. Used by permission.

Cover design by David Meyer; cover image from Stone
Book design by Michelle L. N. Cook

ISBN 0-8066-4354-4

The paper used in this publication meets the minimum requirements of American National Standard for Information Sciences—Permanence of Paper for Printed Library Materials, ANSI Z329.48-1984. ∞ ™

Manufactured in the U.S.A.   AF 9-4354

06   05   04   03   02   1   2   3   4   5   6   7   8   9   10

CONTENTS

Introduction ❧ 5

Chapter 1
Friending ❧ 11

Chapter 2
Faithing ❧ 17

Chapter 3
Cherishing ❧ 23

Chapter 4
Voicing ❧ 29

Chapter 5
Supporting ❧ 34

Chapter 6
Friend-Keeping ❧ 41

Chapter 7
Making Special ❧ 48

Works Cited ❧ 53

INTRODUCTION

Mary and Margaret had been friends for years. As Mary was dying, Margaret came to spend the afternoon with Mary's adult children. One son asked, "How long have you been friends?" Margaret smiled, "I met your mother in 1937—long before you were born. Why, I still remember the day you were born. Your mother and I met at the old church when it was on 24th and Howard." Amazed, the son realized that these two women had been friends for more than six decades.

Margaret and Mary had said goodbye many times at the doors of their homes. Sunday after Sunday the two friends had said, "See you next week." During the week the friends ended their "just-to-talk" phone conversations with, "See you soon."

But one good-bye would be different. Six mornings later, in a parlor at Ratterman & Sons, Margaret stood eulogizing her friend. Then she faced the casket.

"Now Mary, I am older than you. I was supposed to go first. But you have gone ahead. So, I will see you soon." Margaret turned to the mourners. "You will have to excuse me. I need to go see about dinner for this family."

Margaret was my mother's friend. I am still amazed by the longevity of their friendship. I wonder if I will be anyone's six-decade friend. But did anyone tell Margaret that she had a right to grieve? Probably not. After all, she was "just a friend."

We create words for the important experiences of life and relationships. A person who has lost both parents can say, "I am an orphan." A man who has lost his wife can say, "I am a widower." A woman who has lost her husband can say, "I am a widow." A person who has lost a friend, however, has no word to describe the relational loss.

Joseph Roux asks, "That man who has known that immense unhappiness of losing a friend, by what name do we call him?" On this loss, he adds, "Every language holds its peace." Consider the importance of the "best friend" or the "best man" and "maid of honor" at weddings. Why is there no such recognition of friends at funerals?

I am a griever. I am a friendgriever—one who grieves for friends who have died.

I am not a novice. I have reached a point in life where friends' deaths are not uncommon. I first learned about friendgrief from my mother, who often said to me, "Whole lot of people leaving here." I did not comprehend the significance of the words until the year I helped her send Christmas cards; I addressed the envelopes as Mother signed the cards. Since I had moved away after graduating from mortuary school, she had friends I did not know. In the Bs something began to discomfort me; by the Ds, I understood. So many names in that directory—which had laid beside the telephone in my parent's home for as long as I could remember—were crossed out. Deceased. My mother's social network had disintegrated. Mother's observation, "Whole lot of people leaving here" suddenly sounded like a lament.

Ten to twenty million Americans experience the death of a friend in a given year. Yet there is reluctance to recognize friendgrief. For some, the concept of friendgrief is irrelevant. Reviewing my academic text, *Friendgrief: An Absence Called Presence,* one therapist dismissed it outright: "I have been a clinician for thirty years. I have never had anyone with this issue." He knew fathergrief, mothergrief, siblinggrief, childgrief. But friendgrief—what will they think of next?

Grief for a friend is not new. The ancients understood it well—perhaps better than we because they took friendship so seriously. Around the fires, early humans moaned for friends lost to accidents or illness. On blood-soaked battlefields—to this day—soldiers openly grieve for fallen comrades; in war-ravaged villages and towns, survivors openly grieve for lost friends. In the catacombs, the early Christians openly grieved for friends torn to death by wild animals and gladiators. Four millennia ago, the Jewish warrior-king David wailed grief for his friend:

> *I grieve for you, Jonathan;*
> *you were very dear to me.*
> *Your love for me was wonderful,*
> *more wonderful than that of women.*
> (2 Samuel 1:26)

Not only did David compose a lament for his friend, but he "ordered that the men of Judah be taught this lament" (v. 18). Imagine those beefy, testosterone-soaked soldiers sitting around campfires in a sing-along about the death of the king's comrade. Through time, friends have given grief a voice. Have you?

My grandparents and my parents have died. But in actuality, the most troubling losses have been the deaths of my friends, particularly the premature, "Oh, God, no!" deaths. Just writing this brings Cecil to mind. What was God thinking in letting that young college president die! Such unexplainable deaths have caused me to reexamine my beliefs about God and grace, providence and friendship, and, these days, guardian angels. Some deaths are difficult to accept. Kneeling in a cemetery and running my fingers along the letters of a friend's grave marker is sometimes the only way to convince me of its reality.

Although I have been reluctant to use the word *precious* when referring to friendships, some days I find myself auditioning the word. I find myself more willing to be inconvenienced to spend time with friends; disappointed when others do not make the time. Friendship, even in this fast-paced culture, means making time for—and taking time to be with—friends. It means higher long distance telephone bills. Words on a computer screen may be fine—but I want to hear that particular voice, that particular laugh.

As so many learned from the terrorist attacks on New York City and the Pentagon, there may not be a "next time." There is only now time. Precious time.

Friendgrief demands that I acknowledge that, contrary to the notions of a culture in which anyone or anything "can be replaced," a friendship is not replaceable. Commenting on the death of his friend W. H. Auden, whose give name was Wystan, Oliver Sacks wrote, "there is a Wystan-shaped space which will never be filled." New friends cannot be expected to fill the vacuum left by the deaths of old friends.

Wise friends choose to grieve. Wise friends give themselves and others permission to grieve thoroughly— even when society protests, "She was only a friend." (Maybe she was only a friend, but she was *my* friend!)

Wise friends ponder what this loss has to teach about friendship.

Wise friends choose to remember. To say names. To tell stories. To cherish memories.

Wise friends offer doxologies, words of praise for the generous acts of friending.

Wise friends know there is no expiration date on grief for a friend. In time, one reconciles with that significant loss.

Wise friends guard the right to mourn publicly and to be socially supported in grief work.

Wise friends guard the right to maintain continuing bonds with that friend.

Wise friends guard the right to grieve regardless of the social status of the friend or the value assigned to that individual by others.

Wise friends guard the right to hear: "Your grief for a friend counts!"

Wise friends give grief for a friend its voice. By paying attention to your grief for this friend—these friends—you will be a better friend. By doing thorough griefwork you model an enfranchisement that will give others permission to grieve for their friends.

ASSIGNMENT

Give yourself permission to grieve for your friend.

CHAPTER 1

FRIENDING

 The German Navy inflicted havoc on British shipping lanes in the North Sea during the early days of World War I. Critically-needed war supplies were regularly torpedoed until Prime Minister Lloyd George ordered all cargo ships to travel in protected convoys. That order significantly reduced losses and changed naval strategy.

Blessed is an individual with a convoy of dependable friends, both local and long distance. Blessed is an individual with "call-and-I'll-come-running" friends to lend a helping hand when life ambushes. A real friend, writes novelist Elizabeth Berg, "makes me remember who I am, that I am." The American myth of rugged individualism waters down friendship. Even the Lone Ranger had Tonto. But trying to go it alone can be as dangerous as a solo ship crossing the North Sea in 1917.

When someone dies, friends grieve individually and collectively. It is common at visitation or memorial services to hear, "What will we do without . . . ?" But inside, you wonder, "What will *I* do without . . . ?" especially when you reach for the phone to share good news or yet another annoying injustice of contemporary life, only to realize that your friend is no longer there for you.

You grieve your friend in a culture in which many are clueless about establishing, maintaining, and honoring friendships. Many cannot appreciate your level of achieved friendship. Ann Swidler assesses contemporary friendships, "Modern friendship works in part because it isn't so demanding. It's turnonable, and turnoffable. Friends are like a line of credit at the bank, but you don't draw on them all the time." At its worst, this sort of "friendship lite" becomes an accommodation to hectic schedules and a fear of real friendship.

FRIENDSHIP VS. FRIENDLINESS

Have you heard, "It is in times like these that you learn who your real friends are?" Friendliness is often mistaken or substituted for friendship. Many of us settle for friendly acquaintanceships—"Hi. How are you? Nice to see you. Bye!"—and prefer low-risk, low-maintenance friends. Little surprise that many routinely preface requests with, "If it's not asking too much."

Thus, friendships are disposable. When you grieve a friend in a "quickly-find-a-replacement" society, you will be told—or have already been told—"Just get out there and make some new friends." Jane Mansbridge considers friendship "fantastically voluntaristic. . . . I voluntarily enter; I voluntarily leave" when it suits me. Many maintain a friendship only as long as it remains personally beneficial. Some periodically purge their roster of friends in the same way a writer deletes paragraphs from a manuscript.

Increasingly, friends "friend" when it is convenient. "So busy these days . . . would love to see you some time." One question asked in a funeral home or notification call can indict: "When was the last time you saw her?" Friendships take time, energy, and patience— increasingly rare commodities. Funerals remind us of that. It gets our attention but never seems to keep our attention. We leave funerals or memorial services determined to be a better friend and to stay in touch, only to be reminded of that broken promise at the next funeral of a friend. The ancients, like Cicero, would scoff at our watered-down friendships. They might ask, "You call this friendship?" Unfortunately, some do.

Because many friends are too hurried and too stressed to invest time in nurturing friendships, friends drift in and out of our lives. We rely on tiny-fonted Christmas letters or scrawled notes across the bottom of a card to catch us up or keep in touch. The long letters that friends exchanged through history seem quaint in the age of cyber-communication.

THE ABSENCE OF A PRECISE DEFINITION

So, what does *friend* mean to you? I was fascinated by a six-year-old's contribution to a family Christmas letter: "My name is Rachel . . . and I have nine best friends." I found myself simultaneously wondering about Rachel's qualifications for "best" friend and envious of her friending skills.

The *Oxford English Dictionary*'s three pages on friendship illustrates how impoverished our vocabulary has become. We have seen the demise of words like *friendable, friended, friendful, friendstrong, friendess, friendstead,* which now trigger spell check. Such words are archaic because friendships atrophy when people invest less time with friends.

Read through this list of synonyms for friend. What names and faces come to mind in connection with each one?

buddy	crony	pal
amigo	soulmate	true blue friend
mate	girlfriend	old friend
bloke	bosom buddy	sidekick
playmate	best friend	chum
companion	confidante	intimate
personal friend	real friend	close friend

For each match, when was the last time you had a quality conversation or spent quality time with that friend?

Friend is an ambiguous word shaped by the user's and listener's distinct experience with the word. Because we define friendship so loosely, we need modifiers like *best, good,* and *old* to understand someone's use of friend or its many synonyms.

Linguists bemoan this lack of precision in the use of *friend* in contemporary English. Your definition of *friend* might match my definition of *acquaintance.* *Friend* covers everyone from intimates to mere acquaintances. *Friend* functions like an umbrella covering relationships that are anything but a friendship. The phrases "I wouldn't call that a friend" or "Some friend he turned out to be!" are common these days. Adin Steinsaltz contends, "Some unfortunate people have no understanding of the word *friend* beyond the dictionary definition. They have never experienced deep friendship, so they do not even know that it exists, and are therefore missing something in their lives."

Some have no friendships to grieve. When individuals discount or do not understand your grief, consider the possibility that they have never been befriended as you have been.

Sometimes, a "great" friendship illustrates a definition. As part of the 117th birthday celebration for Harry Truman at the Truman Presidential Library, a single yellow rose was placed on Bess Truman's grave. The symbolism was lost on many in the audience. When the former First Lady died in 1982, her longtime friend Mary Paxton Keeley sent a single yellow rose to the service to mark their friendship of ninety years! Although Mrs. Keeley had been an outstanding journalist, there was one topic she never wrote about: her friendship with Bess Wallace Truman. It was too precious to her.

Phyllis Theroux describes friendship in this way:

> Every person is born into a particular quadrant of the heavens. Our friends hang like companion stars around us, giving us point and direction. We run to them when we have something to celebrate, fall back upon them when feeling ill-used or ill-defined.

My friend Barbara Schiller expands on the analogy: "With the friendships I have made over the years, it will never be too dark because my friends are the stars." But how different the sky appears in the absence of that special star. What was life like for Mary Paxton Keeley without Bess? What has life been like for so many New Yorkers after their friends' violent and tragic deaths? You have some idea.

What I know about friendship I have learned from friends. Much of what I know about grief I have learned grieving friends.

ASSIGNMENT
Spend some time reflecting on your definition of friendship.

CHAPTER 2

FAITHING

On a spring day in 1864, an elderly man slowly dropped flower blossoms into a freshly-made grave. His friend Nathaniel Hawthorne had died while they were on a leisurely trip across the New Hampshire countryside. Riding along, they had talked about death, with Hawthorne suggesting, "What a boon it would be, if when life draws to a close, one could pass away without a struggle." Hawthorne died in his sleep that night in exactly that way.

Franklin Pierce, the man dropping blossoms into the grave, had been the fourteenth president of the United States. He was well-acquainted with grief. When his eleven-year-old son was killed en route to the inauguration, and Mrs. Pierce blamed her husband's political aspirations for the death, Hawthorne comforted Pierce. When Pierce returned to New Hampshire after his single term in the White House, many friends turned against him because of his pro-Southern policies.

Not Hawthorne. In December l863, when Mrs. Pierce died, Hawthorne was there, friending Pierce.

The former president was pointedly not asked to be a pallbearer for Hawthorne. But after Emerson, Longfellow, and Whittier—other friends, bearers—had left the cemetery, Pierce remained. In friendgrief, Hawthorne would remain alive in Pierce's memories.

I am grateful that friends are still part of my life—not were but are. I have chosen to make room in my life for a new level of friendship with them. My life, richly blessed by their presence, is now enhanced by their absence. I once agreed with Letty Pogrebin that "Death is friendship's final closure"—a period at the end of a sentence. But my understanding has been challenged by grief scholars, such as Tom Attig, who points to a reality called "continuing bonds." Attig explains:

> Consciously remembering those who have died is the key that opens our hearts, that allows us to love them in new ways. Remembering is not longing. . . . As we remember what we love about those who have died, we welcome them back into our lives even though we are apart.

Death is not a period at the end of sentence . . . it is an ellipsis between sentences. Friends accompany us into the future, for friendship transcends the framework of time past, present, and future.

For years I sang the hymn, "For All the Saints" without giving much thought to the words, without connecting "the saints" to my friends who have died. But there came a moment when, after a friend's funeral, William Walsham How's words took on new meaning:

O blest communion, fellowship divine!
We feebly struggle, they in glory shine;
Yet all are one in Thee, for all are thine.

In the Apostle's Creed we confess, "I believe in the communion of saints"; I admit that I was long unaware of the rich significance of the phrase. The faith that has sustained me in my grief convinces me that we "all are one." There is no great gap between the communion of friends in heaven and friends on earth. I have every expectation that someday my companions and I will resume our conversations: "Sorry for the interruption. Now, where were we?"

GOD GIVES ETERNAL LIFE

When I was a child I memorized the scripture, "In my father's house are many mansions. . . . I go to prepare a place for you. And if I go to prepare a place for you, I will come again, and receive you unto myself; that where I am, there ye may be also" (John 14:2-3 KJV). Jesus' words to his friends are words to you and to your friends as well. As a fifth grader memorizing those red-lettered words, I could not appreciate them—just a strung collection of words to fulfill a teacher's assignment. But those words have become a "faith jacket" that I wear always.

The shortest verse in scripture— "Jesus wept" (John 11:35)—is brief enough for anyone to memorize. The Biblical author felt no need to expand beyond its elegant simplicity: Jesus wept when his friend Lazarus died. Jesus not only wept, but was "deeply moved and troubled in spirit" (John 11:33). This incident offers us all permission to grieve.

GOD BRINGS FRIENDS TOGETHER

I cannot forget the confidence of one participant in my doctoral research. When I asked, "Do you believe you will see your friend again?" his "Oh yes!" was resounding. When I asked why, he answered, "Why would God go to all that trouble to bring us together as friends, if he didn't have something longer in mind?" Why indeed? In the third century, Augustine of Hippo concluded, "There is no true friendship, Lord, except between those whom you bind together." He encouraged friends, "Blessed are those who love you, Lord, and their friends in you, and their enemies also, for your sake. For they are the only ones who will never lose anyone dear to them, since all who are dear to them in you, our God, and can never be lost."

Thomas Jefferson set aside some of his beliefs

about eternity to comfort his "deeply afflicted friend" John Adams. In his writings, he predicted "an ecstatic meeting with the friends we have loved and lost and whom we shall still love and never lose again." If only these words of Jefferson were as well known as "We hold these truths to be self-evident. . . ."

The Gallup Organization reports that most Americans believe in some form of existence after death. A friend's death often initiates a thorough audit of our beliefs in life after death; sometimes, as for Jefferson, existing perspectives must accommodate new longings. C. S. Lewis, after the devastating death of his close friend Charles Williams, wrote, "No event has so corroborated my faith in the next world as Williams did simply by dying. When the idea of death and the idea of Williams thus met in my mind, it was the idea of death that was changed."

GOD DOES NOT ERASE OUR MEMORIES

Friends, although dead, periodically wander the corridors of our hearts. A song, a scent, a photo, a "remember the time?" brings them back. They are not "gone," nor have we "lost them," as long as they are in our hearts and stories. You learned so much from them in life, why shouldn't you learn from them in absentia? In fact, by witnessing the dying of some friends, some of us become less afraid to die. How many times did a friend say before some adventure, "Okay, I'll go first, then you"?

I thought I knew so much about friendgrief, but this book has been influenced by the death of a close friend. Billy died around the time I began writing. I am again wandering a wilderness for which Fodor offers no guidebook. I write with a Billy-shaped hole in my heart.

I appreciate what the nineteenth-century preacher Dwight Moody wrote to friends. "By and by you will hear people say, 'Mr. Moody is dead.' Don't believe a word of it—for at that very moment, I shall be more alive than I am now. I shall then truly begin to live."

When I grieve for Billy, I must remember that Billy is more alive than he ever was. Billy is more Billy than he has ever been. Billy is Billy in a new limitless eternal edition. The same with your friend.

One of our greatest gifts is the belief in reunion. Hope in reunion is grief's greatest resource. In the days of American slavery, slaves sang a confident anticipation of reunion with friends. Spirituals such as "Swing Low, Sweet Chariot" have comforted friends for generations.

If you get there before I do
Coming for to carry me home;
Tell all my friends, I'm coming too
Coming for to carry me home.

ASSIGNMENT

Do your friend one last favor: mourn for him, grieve for her.

CHAPTER 3

CHERISHING

 Jim Moore, a New York restaurateur, cherished his many friends in the theatrical world. Friends who died were greatly missed by Moore as he got older. One afternoon as he visited the graves of several friends, remonstrating with them for their thoughtlessness in dying, he thumped George M. Cohan's headstone with a fresh fish. "In case you don't know," he shouted, "today's Friday, and I just want you to see what you're missing."

Cherishing is an important gift of grace by a friend. You honor a friend when you cherish memories. Webster defines *cherish* as "to hold dear . . . to keep or cultivate with care and affection; to entertain or harbor in the mind deeply and resolutely." Cherishing is like my mother and grandmother planning a quilt. Garments that had been loved but were well-worn were cut into pieces and stuffed into a large bag. Eventually they pulled fabric pieces from the bag and began trying out patterns for a future quilt—a process Hawaiians call *humuhumu,* fitting the pieces together. In cherishing, you "quilt" memories that can warm your soul, you honor your friend, and you keep her present.

CHERISH BY REMEMBERING

Remembering is one way we carry friends into the future. I ask dying friends, "How do you want me to remember you?" When friends die without warning, I convene a committee of the heart to formulate a working plan for remembrance. Cherishing comes when we make room and offer hospitality to the memories.

If you were to wander my heart you would think it a museum of friendship. I cherish particular memories with all the enthusiasm of a museum curator displaying a masterpiece. If you visit my home, you find artifacts of friendships. For example, I have a cross made of two glass nails—a gift from the estate of a friend. It is priceless to me because my friend wanted me to have something of his. When I see it, I hear ancient words—words that friends have shared with friends throughout the centuries—spoken in a soft Georgia accent: Remember me.

CHERISH BY REMEMBERING REALISTICALLY

Healthy grievers reconcile with a friend's death by recollecting and reexperiencing the deceased and the friendship realistically. Some grievers have to grapple with a friend's shadow. The superstition, "Speak no ill of the dead" discourages honest memory making. You can acknowledge your friend's worst faults but still cherish his memory. Remember the real friend— "warts and all." None of us are exempt from fault.

CHERISH BY TELLING STORIES

A person is not gone until friends stop telling stories about her, or edit him out of stories. Here's a Billy story I cherish:

Our friendship began in a most unfriendly act at dinner with a group of college admissions counselors. At the time, I weighed 275 pounds. As I reached for my pie, Billy, a stranger, blocked it with his hand: "You know, you don't need to eat that!" Never in the next twenty-five years did he apologize. That act of brashness led to many more conversations and, in time, I became more responsible for my eating.

You cherish when you tell stories about a friend— and you promote your own psychological well-being when you remember to remember. Pretend that I am seated across from you. Tell me a story about your friend.

CHERISH BY USING TECHNOLOGY

Early one morning, while jogging past the repository in Canton, Ohio, I noticed a plaque near the entrance that said, "Memory is the dearest friend now." These words were written by a friend of President William McKinley after his assassination in 1903. The sentence reminds me that memory is our ally, not our enemy. With our technology—particularly video and computers—we possess enormous tools for stockpiling a repository of memories. Karen cherished by creating a Web site honoring her friend Ryan. Greg cherished by putting together a cassette of his friend Martin's favorite music. At the memorial service, the playing of that cassette evoked smiles and tears. For a few moments, Martin was "there," singing, because any song on the radio was an invitation for him to sing.

CHERISH BY ACTIVE REMEMBERING

Some friends go along with cherishing if you bring it up, but prefer more passive remembering. Someone often becomes the designated "rememberer" in a circle of friends. Who in your friend network will be guardian of the stories?

Cherishing can happen spontaneously as two friends eat in a small bistro in Paris and one remarks, "Wouldn't John have loved this place?" That act of cherishing becomes more treasured when a friend responds and ups the ante, "Yes, he would have. What was the name of that greasy burger place he loved?" When forks go down and glasses come up for a toast, a friend is being cherished and the raw material for a future cherished memory is made.

THANKS FOR THE MEMORIES

You cherish when you offer hospitality to a memory that has wandered into your consciousness. Comedian Bob Hope's theme song was entitled, "Thanks for the Memories." When I see friends again, as I believe I shall, I want them to be able to say, "You remembered. You cherished."

You cherish when you:
- drop tears or stoop to touch a grave marker
- place notes or pictures or poems at a roadside memorial where a friend died
- wear a ribbon highlighting the cause of death
- challenge storytellers, "Don't leave out the part about . . ."
- take condolences and stories to visitations and memorial services
- offer stories that family members and other friends do not know
- honor Memorial Day and All Souls' Day
- create impromptu cherish moments

Cherishing is enhanced when you revisit places of importance, view photos or videos, tell stories, or solicit stories from other friends. Go to a favorite shared place and be hospitable to the memories that show up. Invite a memory to "sit a spell." Something wonderful can happen when memory boots up and says, "Remember the time . . . ?"

ASSIGNMENT

Find a creative way to cherish the memory of your friend.

CHAPTER 4

VOICING

 The tributes for a well-known actor, staged in the first theater in which the man had worked, had been dramatic. Then, an unscheduled speaker walked onto the stage. It was the theater's custodian. As he described a friendship "out of the spotlight," the theater grew quiet. Finished, he quickly exited the stage. Spontaneously, the audience stood and applauded.

> Had someone walked in at that moment, he would have seen what seemed like a group of slightly deranged artists applauding an empty stage. But everyone knew that the stage was fuller than it had ever been before.

Why? Because a friend gave grief a voice.

As grievers we all have three needs: to find the words for the loss, to say the words aloud, and to know that the words have been heard.

FIND THE WORDS FOR THE LOSS

In order to give grief its voice, a friend tries out words. Initially, it is not surprising that you may be speechless or find words inadequate. That reality keeps Hallmark in business as a source of borrowed words.

How do I find the words to capture such a friend? Talking about loss is like being kidnapped and taken to another culture and forced to communicate. Marc Gafni suggests that a eulogy "should be an attempt to do in death what we are so often unable to do in life— to portray so accurately and lovingly as possible the measure of a person's depths."

TO SAY THE WORDS ALOUD

To put into words and phrases what other mourners only think makes memorable eulogies. I have attended "generic" funerals where the deceased was all but personalityless, at least from the minister's perspective. Then I have watched friends shift out of automatic pilot, as a friend walked to the podium, unfolded a piece of paper, shifted nervously, fumbled with the microphone, and announced, "I am not much of a speaker," but then offered a eulogy so stunning that friends wrapped their fingers around the words and carried them away.

To Know that Your Words have been Heard

Some families want persons known to be "good with words" to offer the eulogy. I own several fine books of eulogies; the tables of contents read like a "who's who" of orators and wordsmiths. But I know that exquisite eulogies may be spoken by apologetic friends. Eloquent words have been known to tumble out when a friend spontaneously stands and says, "I just want to say this about my friend. . . ." Sometimes, there is a significant time delay before the words are appreciated.

Incredible eulogies are delivered at the coffee machine in a lounge at a funeral home, in the parking lot, or while eating chicken and potato salad after the service. Marvelous eulogies are whispered between friends standing near caskets, or six weeks later when friends call to ask "how are you doing?" Eulogies show up along the corridors of our hearts in quiet bedrooms, when sleep will not come, as friends put grief into words. Some have listeners in those sacred moments; some do not. But friends drift to sleep, comforted that finally grief has been expressed.

Your Eulogy Could Be a Model

When my friend Dana Walling died in 2000, Dean Nelson faced a challenge. Because he is a journalist who makes his living arranging words, the gathered cohort of friends expected a lot. Besides, Dana was no run-of-the-mill friend. Dean began, "As one can imagine, I have done considerable thinking about Dana Walling in recent months—especially these last few weeks and days. I started compiling what I call: Some Unique Dana Moments."

Nelson described sailing off the coast of San Diego, when a group of friends found themselves in a thick fog bank. One ordered Dana to stand at the bow and to shout if they were about to hit anything. Dana took the task seriously, stretching both hands out into the fog.

"There we were, plowing through the water, with Dana leading us through the dark and fog. . . . We eventually arrived safely, laughed nervously, and hugged each other, grateful that we made it together."

Using that story as an anchor, Nelson concluded:

That's kind of how I feel about these last few months. Dana's the only one who could see a little bit ahead through the fog. We all trusted that he could see enough, and he led the way. He had already shown us how to live. Now he was showing us how to die. None of us can see very far ahead, but we watched Dana as he showed us that what we have is enough to get us home. Eventually, we will all arrive, and we'll laugh and hug and be grateful that we're back together.

A friend's words were heard that summer afternoon and continue to be heard. Years from now, I think worn-out copies of Dean's eulogy will be found among the personal effects of friends who cherished Dana.

It's Never too Late for a Eulogy

You eulogize friends whenever you tell their stories. Maybe you weren't up to doing a eulogy at the time of the funeral or memorial service. A friend can eulogize in a poem written months later or in words scrawled across a sympathy card. A friend can eulogize with words in a Christmas letter. A friend can write a eulogy and read it at the grave. Elegant eulogies often begin, "I will always remember the time my friend. . . ." Eulogies are composed and voiced after a meal, when the plates are pushed back and friends reminisce. Consider these words of eulogy crafted by a friend:

> I had often heard people speak of burying a part of themselves with some friend, parent, or spouse; but I never had cause to reflect upon the truth hidden in what sounded like a maudlin cliché. Life goes on, right? Of course it does. But when you lose somebody who remembers who and what you were in fifth grade, you do bury a part of your life, a part of your history.

A eulogy is not simply "putting in your two cents worth." Eulogy can be a sacred act through which friends give grief a voice.

Assignment

Re-eulogize your friend.

CHAPTER 5

SUPPORTING

In the aftermath of the terrorist attack on the World Trade Center, retired NFL player Boomer Esiason attended many of funerals—too many. Among these was the funeral of his best friend, Timmy O'Brien, whom Esiason eulogized while wearing the jersey of O'Brien's number-one team, the New York Giants. So many funerals were a challenge for Esiason. Like so many other grieving friends, he assumed that after so many funerals, the tears would stop.

Esiason took a lot of physical punishment on football fields as quarterback for the New York Jets and other teams. But attending funerals entailed a different kind of pain. "You cry for each one. You have pain in your gut for each and every one." Dropping his children off at school one morning, Esiason was stunned to learn that a neighbor was facing seventeen funerals in one week.

"Every time I go to a service, I cry for that family, and I cry for Timmy, and I cry for every other family whose service I've attended."

But who supported Esiason as he trudged through the emotional equivalent of bumper cars? Who supports you? Who periodically asks, "How are you doing?" and weighs your response before asking, "How are you really doing?"

Who supported Esiason?

That's What Friends Are For

Friends are expected to provide physical, emotional, and sometimes financial support. Some consider friends who fail to "be there" or to "come through" for the family to be betraying the friendship. Yet, these days, with friends scattered to the four winds, what level of support is realistic? Admittedly, some friends "mothball" their own grief in order to concentrate energies and resources into supporting the family. But friends discover that unattended grief accumulates like compound interest. Nina Donnelley challenges this disenfranchisement. "When we lose someone or something we love, we have a right to mourn. And, regardless, we will mourn. . . . After all, your friend is worth being mourned, is she not?"

THE CHIEF SUPPORTER

In the event of death, there is often a need for a friend to step in and, on the family's behalf, manage details and coordinate support. This organizer, or chief supporter, asks, What needs to be done now? Who can do it?

The chief supporter recruits and coordinates support, communicates, interprets, cajoles, and occasionally negotiates the wishes of the chief mourner or family in regard to friends in the extended social network. Friends sometime find this a thankless job that leaves them emotionally and physically exhausted or at odds with other friends. Being an in-the-background manager of the numerous details can be a huge undertaking—a reality that points to the origin of the word *undertaker*.

THE FRIEND AS GRIEVER

Historically, because families stand to inherit, societal norms have mandated that friends not compete with, overshadow, challenge, undermine, or complicate the family's grief. Friends may feel pressured to keep their grief to themselves rather than express it in a way that might interfere with the grieving of the family. Many friends think their only line in this pageant is, "Never mind my grief." As a friend, you may discount—even camouflage—your grief in order to support the family; but self-disenfranchisement complicates your own ability to reconcile with the death. Every time you say,

"Oh, don't worry about me, I'm fine," you wound your soul.

The Old Testament provides a narrative of the supportive friendship between Jonathan and David. When King Saul was trying to kill his son's best friend, "Saul's son Jonathan went to David at Horesh and helped him find strength in God" (1 Samuel 23:16). While every friend has an equivalent of Horesh, not everyone has a friend to help find "strength in God." Sometimes help is a hug, a call, a hand on the shoulder, shared moments over coffee, or a simple statement recognizing that, "You were close, weren't you?"

You may not recognize your emotional reactions as grief. You may be so busy caring for the family that you ignore your grief or the grief of other friends. "Making support" can become a socially-sanctioned distraction from fully acknowledging loss.

FAMILIES ACCOMMODATING FRIENDGRIEF

Some families are open to support; others consider death a time for "circling the wagons" and viewing friends as outsiders or intruders. Friends' offers of hospitality may be sifted for hidden motives. Some friends think that anything less than full, unquestioned cooperation with the family betrays friendship. Thus, families have been known to take advantage of the generosity of friends, sometimes prefaced by, "You've done so much, I hate to ask this, but could you . . . ?"

For some friends, no request is too much, especially if you promised at the funeral home, "Just let me know if there is anything I can do." Such a statement is often a polite cliché when you do not know what else to say, but some listeners will consider those words the equivalent of a coupon to be clipped and redeemed. How readily will you honor it?

Sometimes tensions develop among friends over expectations of support. You may be annoyed by a friend who did not pitch in or assume her fair share (or the share you consider fair). Some friends go into hyper mode as a way of numbing themselves, or to atone for being unavailable in previous times of need.

DEFINING EXPECTATIONS OF SUPPORT

How much a family expects of friends—or a certain friend—is shaped by their appreciation of friendship as well as by their personal experience with grief. Local customs also influence expectations. A friend's family lived in an isolated farming community where everyone pitched in. Our extended friend network could not meet the family's expectations (or "demands," according to some in the network). You may feel guilty—or have been made to feel guilty—because you did not meet expectations for support. Ask yourself: Were those expectations realistic?

I answer that question by consulting my own core of expectations. A friend:

- calls the family or goes to the residence upon learning of the death
- sends a sympathy card and flowers unless a "no flowers" decision has been made
- donates to a designated charity
- attends the visitation or wake, the memorial service or funeral, and the burial or scattering
- prepares or donates food for the family
- promises future assistance: "If there is anything I can do, please call"
- fulfills specific family requests such as "Could you take this dress to the cleaners?"

When specifically invited by the chief mourner, a friend may:
- supply any missing data he needs to know
- offer advice on decisions: "What do you think we should do about . . . ?"
- participate in the rituals or deliver a eulogy
- serve as a casket, pall, or urn bearer

Friends were once directly involved with washing and preparing the body, building a casket, digging a grave, and so on. As these tasks have been assumed by funeral directors, friends have been relegated to a passive, secondary status. Two generations ago, no one had to say, "If there is anything I can do, let me know," because there was plenty to be done. These days, many friends feel like extras on a movie set.

FRIENDS AS SUPPORT MAGICIANS

Women often feel particular pressure to be caregivers to the grieving. The large movement of women into the workplace, however, has had a significant impact on the time and energy they have had available to be "support magicians." Some wear themselves down "trying to do it all." But wise load-bearers are load-sharers. Healthy friends ask for and receive support. Don't overlook your own need for care.

Jesus, facing his darkest hour, recruited his three closest friends—Peter, James, and John—to support him. Despite repeated requests, they failed to come through. So "An angel from heaven appeared to him and strengthened him" (Mark 22:43). Apparently, the writer of the traditional Appalachian folk song never found strength through friends or an "angel" because he wrote, "You've got to walk that lonesome valley, you've got to walk it by yourself. Nobody else can walk it for you."

There may be none who can walk it for you, but perhaps an angel, disguised as a friend, can walk it with you.

ASSIGNMENT

Give yourself permission to receive support.

FRIEND-KEEPING

 Kansas City was abuzz with speculation and rumor. Thomas J. Pendergast—the political boss who had ruled Kansas City, rewarding friends, punishing enemies, until the Feds had busted him for tax evasion—had died. Just the week before, one of his friends had taken the oath of office as the vice president of the United States. The question at the wake was: Would he come? Yes, of course, some argued, he was Tom's friend. Others countered that he would not, now that he was vice president.

Vice President Harry Truman's statement, "He was always my friend and I have always been his," ran in a story in *The Kansas City Star.* Republicans were hoping Truman would show up because they could rekindle allegations that the Democrat Truman was Pendergast's "stooge." If "a man is known by the company he keeps," the vice president had a lot to explain.

The morning of the funeral, the seven hundred seats in Visitation Catholic Church filled quickly. As 10:00 A.M. approached, some whispered, "Truman isn't coming," while others fumed, "Some friend he turned out to be!" But at 9:50 A.M. a twin engine Army bomber touched down at the Kansas City municipal airport. Harry Truman climbed out and dashed to a waiting car.

As the Rev. Edward J. Taney tried to close the church doors, a car screeched to a halt at the curb. When Truman emerged, Father Taney escorted Truman down the aisle to a front pew. "He's here!" "It's him!"

The reactions were predictable. Some expressed admiration for Truman because he ignored the politically expedient course of action, while some grumbled about an unthinkable disgrace of a sitting vice president attending the funeral of a shady character. Thirty years later, Truman reminisced:

> You should have heard the squawks. Headlines in the newspapers and editorials and I don't know what all. And they said some very mean things, but I didn't care. I couldn't have done anything else. What kind of man would it be . . . [who] wouldn't go to his friend's funeral because he'd be criticized for it? [7]

FRIEND-KEEPERS: EXPERTS ON LOSS

"Sooner or later," says Rabbi David Wolpe, "every one of us becomes an expert on loss." Even vice presidents.

Sometimes, on the anvil of friendgrief rather than familygrief, you gain expertise on grief. Wolpe tells of an elderly woman whose friends had all died. Asked what she missed most, this survivor friend answered, "There is no one to call me Rosie anymore." No friend with whom to share the inside joke. No friend to remember the time when. . . . No one to call and say, "I need your prayers. . . ." No friend to encourage, "Oh, go ahead. . . ."

In a moving column in the Memorial Day 2001 *Kansas City Star,* Dennis Hanners reminded readers of the importance of "this day of memory " by relating the story of his buddy, Gary Butt. Gary had already lost best friends in Vietnam, but seemed unhardened by the war. Hanners and Butt became friends. Then, days before his twenty-fifth birthday, Gary died carrying a wounded buddy to safety.

We have so many words for trivial things in our culture, but there is no word for Hanners, who has not forgotten his friend, or Truman, who did not forget his. Perhaps *friend-keeper* is the best word. Through stories, we keep our friends alive. Hanners, for example, introduced his friend to thousands of readers and invited them to "keep" their friends as well.

Many grievers, over time, come to share the conviction of John Masius that "Death ends a life, but it doesn't end a relationship." My grandfather Eckert often sang at funerals in his Indiana farming community. As a child I was never surprised when he would interrupt a story about a friend to sing one of his "heaven" songs: "I will meet you in the morning, just inside the Eastern gate. . . ." To my grandfather, his friends were waiting for him at the rendezvous point: heaven's Eastern gate.

The Language of Friend-keeping

There are times, in grief, when I reclaim the vocabulary of my grandfather's songs. Immediately upon learning of my friend Rusty's death, I sat down on the steps and cried. From deep in my consciousness came a song my grandfather sang, "Land where we'll never grow old." I have no idea how long I sat there. I sang until I could not remember any more words. I cried until I was cried out. We have, by and large, discarded as maudlin that tradition of funeral songs, which gave friends permission to sing grief. Strong men like my grandfather—who dug a grave for many a friend—felt no shame in wiping away tears or singing from memory because they could not see the hymnal through their tears. After burying friends, they walked away from cemeteries less burdened than we do.

Friends need language to wrap around a fresh grief. The day Rusty died, language from my childhood comforted me. Rusty will never grow old. His pace will never slow. He will never lose that red hair. He will never lose that vitality.

For many adults, friendgrief is an occasional intrusion; for others, a continual intruder. Grief for a friend unfolds on its own time framework. Five years after the Oklahoma City bombing, Peggy Broxterman dismisses any notion of closure. "You close on a house. You don't close on a death." But you can make decisions that encourage reconciliation with your friend's death.

FRIEND-KEEPING AGAINST ALL ODDS

Sometimes friend-keeping seems to be an inconvenience.

There weren't many tire tracks in the cemetery that frigid day. Because of the seven-inch snowfall, I could have postponed going, but I have a Christmas Eve tradition of visiting friends' graves. I was not prepared for the markers to be covered in a blanket of snow. Not to worry, though. I had been there so many times the grave would be easy to find. Hardly. Soon my gloves were wet, my hands frozen as I tried spot after spot, brushing away the snow. Finally, the letter L emerged. Then Lunn. Then the entire name, M. E. "Bud" Lunn. I placed a tiny artificial tree on the corner of the marker and packed snow around as I recalled Bud's laugh, his belief in me, and his "just a little something for you" Christmas gifts. I had been blessed to be a recipient of his gracious definition of friendship.

I had not been able to to get back to Kansas City for Bud's funeral. I've watched the video, but it is not the same. I missed my friend's funeral. So I keep the friendship by stopping by my friend's resting place every Christmas Eve.

It is often only after—sometimes long after—the death of a friend that we begin to recognize the roles that the person played in our life and the gifts he or she brought to us. Prolonged absence helps us fully appreciate the friendship. Discovery may come long after others have seemingly finished or abandoned their grief and now insist that you, too, move on.

Comedians Alan Zweibel and Gilda Radner were tight friends for fourteen years. Five years after her death, Zweibel confessed, "I don't know if I'm supposed to celebrate the fact that Gilda was in my life, or feel cheated that she's not there anymore." I think the answer is yes to both feelings. But in remembering Gilda, Zweibel is an excellent example of a friend-keeper. He seemed to know, instinctively, that by writing the story of his friendship with Gilda, their relationship, "despite death, is still very much alive."

We will never know exactly what happened on United Flight 93 after it left Newark Airport on the morning of September 11, 2001. Apparently, the terrorists encountered passengers like Mark Bingham, a strapping 220-pound, six-foot-five athlete and public relations firm owner, who thwarted their attempt to reach their apparent destination, a Washington landmark. Within hours after the plane crashed in rural Pennsylvania, friends on both coasts began their lament for Mark, as did friends of other passengers. A memorial sprang up on a sidewalk in front of a bank in San Francisco. A friend of mine visited this shrine and snapped a picture that has captured my heart. On a plain sheet of paper someone wrote:

Mark Bingham
You will be missed. I have always valued your friendship.
You are also the first hero that I have known, and a true one at that.
Rest in peace.

None of the friends that I grieve died at the hand of terrorists that tragic September morning. But lots of friends did. *The New York Times* has run a series of biographical profiles of the victims. I am moved by the fact that the friends mourned by so many others are persons I would like to have called a friend as well.

My friends, dead, gone ahead, were heroes in their own ways. And they still are, in Zweibel's words, "very much alive" in my heart.

Give your grief a voice. Feel cheated that they are now absent. But always, always celebrate their presence in your life. That is friend-keeping.

ASSIGNMENT

Allow your friendship to be "still very much alive." Become a friend-keeper.

CHAPTER 7

MAKING SPECIAL

Pastor Thomas Melton faced a decision that frigid winter day. No one had come to the funeral home to pay respects to the elderly veteran. No one had attended the funeral. Why not bury the man and get out of the cold? As he was about to leave, a car entered that section of the cemetery. Recognizing the car, Melton walked over to speak to its elderly passenger. "You shouldn't be out in weather like this. Please don't get out of the car." But the passenger was determined, so Melton conducted the committal standing beside the car. At the "Amen," he turned and asked his one-man congregation what had brought him out on such a frigid day.

"Pastor, I never forget a friend," Harry Truman answered. The 82-year-old former president of the United States had come to say goodbye to a war buddy.

I've had a lot of practice with friendgrief. I have stood under the tent too many times. The friend-shaped holes in my heart will not heal in my lifetime, even if I should get fourscore and ten. I reviewed those griefs driving six hundred miles home from Dorothy Culver's funeral. We became friends after my friend John, her son, died. Dot had never been afraid of the world. Five times she had been to that cemetery in West Lafayette, Indiana: to bury a father, a mother, a newborn, her husband, and John. Family and friends gathered that Monday after Thanksgiving for her committal heard words that had been recited thousands of times in that cemetery.

The Culvers have never believed in being boring—even at funerals. So, slowly, plastic containers of glitter were passed among mourners under the tent. As the ritual ended, we walked to the casket and let glitter sift through our gloves onto our friend's casket. Then we dusted John Marquis Culver's grave with glitter, too. I was keeping promises made to John as he was dying—promises I make to all my friends:

I will remember you.
I will say your name.
I will tell stories about you.
I will find creative ways to remember our friendship.

John's friends remember with glitter. Dot said, more than once, on visits to that sacred space, "Oh look, glitter. One of John's friends has been here." Which translates: one of John's friends has remembered.

Dot lived ninety-three years (and lived is an understatement, considering camel rides in her seventies and exotic ports of call). Because she had outlived so many inner-circle friends, some wondered how many might attend her services. But Dot was a practitioner of intentional friending. She knew how to make friends. When she broke her hip, she moved to a Mennonite retirement community near her daughter Nancy. That meant saying goodbye to West Lafayette, where she had lived her entire life, but hello to Goshen. As soon as she discovered Purdue alumni living in the retirement community, it became something of a northern suburb of West Lafayette!

Friends came bearing Dot stories. We filled the pews of a historic church where, as a child, Dot had witnessed the Ku Klux Klan's attempt to intimidate parishioners. Friends wiped tears as her granddaughter Alison celebrated the life of a one who had "lived well and friended much." Friends broke into smiles as we recognized the recessional: the Purdue University Fight Song. (Dot was a boilermaker's boilermaker. When Nancy questioned its appropriateness for a funeral, I said, "Do it! It is a way to make it special. We're not burying just anyone—we're celebrating Dot Culver!")

After I returned home some questioned me: "You drove all that way for a *friend?*" What a sad commentary about our busyness in a "let's get together sometime" world. Some are "too busy" to drive across town, let alone six hundred miles, for a friend's funeral. "Hardly anybody there" is a sad assessment of our friendship rosters.

I was glad that I had made a "sometime" three weeks earlier with Dot—never suspecting that the party for Dot on the other side would begin so soon. As I drove, I revisited wonderful conversations we had, especially about the Monon Railroad and her early teaching experiences.

WADING THE WIDE RIVER

I believe death is wading a river into the real country, the bank lined with friends who have gone ahead. And as we wade across, they cheer us on. Dot was no sooner on that shore when she exclaimed her traditional greeting, "Well, look who's here! " Dot was surrounded and hugged and the conversations resumed. The laughter of Dot and family and friends clearly could be heard above the music in the eternal town.

Grief is really a form of doxology—for the blessing of having such a friend (admittedly some will want to insert *had* into that sentence).

The stories about Harry Truman and his commitment to friend-keeping influenced my decision to attend Dot's funeral. Just as I was influenced by Truman's choices, your decision to grieve, to attend, to be doxological in expressing grief, could influence someone else.

Yesterday, I took time from writing this book to slip into a pew alongside a company of friends gathered to celebrate the life of one man and the resurrection of one who radically redefined friendship. One who calls the likes of us *friends*. In words like those that friends have repeated for centuries, we gave grief a voice:

> God of grace and glory, today in your presence we remember our friend.
>
> You gave him to us to know and love on our pilgrimage on earth, and we thank you for him.
>
> In your infinite compassion, console us.
>
> Give us faith to see that death is the door to eternal life.
>
> Give us the confidence to continue our way on earth until you call us and reunite us with those who have gone before.
>
> Through Christ our Lord.
>
> Amen

Ah, reunited.

ASSIGNMENT

Find ways to express exuberant gratitude for having such a friend.

WORKS CITED

INTRODUCTION

Joseph Roux in John Cook, compiler, *The Book of Positive Quotations* (Minneapolis: Fairview Press, 1997), p. 89.

Oliver Sacks in Stephen Spender, ed., *W. H. Auden: A Tribute* (New York: Macmillan), p. 193.

CHAPTER 1

Elizabeth Berg, *Open House: A Novel* (New York: Random House, 2000), p. 150.

Ann Swidler, quoted in Ellen Goodman and Patricia O'Brien, *I Know Just What You Mean: The Power of Friendship in Women's Lives* (New York: Simon and Schuster Trade, 2000), p. 211.

Jane Mansbridge, quoted in Goodman and O'Brien, pp. 211-212.

Adin Steinsaltz in *Simple Words* (New York: Simon and Schuster, 2001), p. 161.

Phyllis Theroux from *The Book of Eulogies* (New York: Simon and Schuster, 1997), p. 279.

CHAPTER 2

"What a boon it would be . . ." from James R. Mellow, *Nathaniel Hawthorne in His Times* (New York: Houghton Mifflin, 1980), p. 577. Other information on Pierce and Hawthorne is drawn from Brian Lamb and the C-SPAN staff, *Who's Buried in Grant's Tomb?* (Baltimore: John Hopkins University Press, 2000), p. 59.

Letty Pogrebin, *Among Friends* (New York: McGraw-Hill, 1986), p. 104.

Robert Attig, *The Heart of Grief* (New York: Oxford University Press, 2000), p. 27.

"For All the Saints" from Bert Polman et al., eds., *Amazing Grace: Hymn Texts for Devotional Use* (Louisville, Ky.: Westminster John Knox Press, 1995), p. 293.

Augustine of Hippo from *Confessions, Book 4,* paraphrased by Harold Ivan Smith.

Thomas Jefferson, quoted in Fawn M. Brodie, *Thomas Jefferson: An Intimate History* (New York: Norton, W. W. & Company, 1974), p. 452.

C. S. Lewis from Dorothy Sayers et al., *Essays Presented to Charles Williams* (Stratford, N. H.: Ayer Company Publishers, Inc., 1977), p. xiv.

Dwight Moody, quoted in George Sweeting, "D. L. Moody: His Steps to Excellence," *Moody Monthly,* February 1985, p. 32.

CHAPTER 3

Jim Moore anecdote from Clifton Fadiman, ed., *The Little Brown Book of Anecdotes* (London: Little, Brown, and Company, 1985), p. 133.

CHAPTER 4

"Had someone walked in . . ." from Marc Gafni, *Soul Prints: Your Path to Fulfillment* (New York: Simon and Schuster, 2001), p. 112.

Mare Gafni, from *Soul Prints,* p. 110.

"I had often heard people speak . . ." from Terry Golway, "Life in the 90s," *America,* July 5, 1997, p. 4.

CHAPTER 5

Boomer Esiason, summarized from Jill Lieber, "Wellspring of tears hasn't run dry," *USA Today,* Sept. 28, 2001.

Nina Donnelly from *I Never Know What to Say* (New York: Random House, 1987), pp. 171-172

CHAPTER 6

"Kansas City was abuzz . . ." originally printed in *The Director,* September 2001 issue, by the National Funeral Director's Association.

"He was always my friend . . ." from an Associated Press article in *The Kansas City Star,* Jan. 27, 1945.

"You should have heard the squawks. . ." from Merle Miller, *Plain Speaking: An Oral Biography of Harry S. Truman* (New York: Random House, 1985), p. 196.

Rabbi David Wolpe from *Making Loss Matter: Creating Meaning in Difficult Times* (New York: Putnam Publishing Group, 1999), p. 5.

"There is no one to call me Rosie anymore," ibid.

John Masius, quoted in Ellen Gray, "Fear not death on TV, for characters usually come back to life," in *The Kansas City Star,* May 29, 2001.

Peggy Broxterman, quoted in *Newsweek,* May 7, 2001, p. 21.

Alan Zweibel from *Bunny Bunny: Gilda Radner, A Sort of Love Story* (New York: Random House, 1994), p. 189 and p. vii.

CHAPTER 7

Pastor Thomas Melton, summarized from Joe Popper, "Vow forged unforeseeable link," in *The Kansas City Star,* June 15, 1996.

OTHER RESOURCES FROM AUGSBURG